Pieces to Play

with

Step by Step

by

Edna Mae Burnam

To my grandson, David Bender

CONTENTS

Book
ISBN 978-1-4234-3595-2

Book/CD
ISBN 978-1-4234-3612-6

WILLIS MUSIC

Exclusively Distributed By

HAL•LEONARD®
CORPORATION
7777 W. BLUEMOUND RD. P.O. BOX 13819 MILWAUKEE, WI 53213

Visit Hal Leonard Online at
www.halleonard.com

TO THE TEACHER

The pieces in this book have been composed to correlate exactly with the Edna Mae Burnam Piano Course STEP BY STEP—Book Two. Prefixed to each piece is an indication of the exact page of STEP BY STEP—Book Two at which a selection from PIECES TO PLAY may be introduced. When the student reaches this page, he/she is ready to play with ease and understanding.

All of the pieces in this book may serve as repertoire for the student at this level.

The pieces in this book should be:

1. Perfected;
2. Memorized;
3. Played with expression and poise;
4. Kept in readiness to play for company.

Edna Mae Burnam

The student is ready to play this piece when he has reached page 13 of
Edna Mae Burnam's STEP BY STEP - Book Two.

A CANYON DEEP

BY EDNA MAE BURNAM

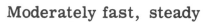

Moderately fast, steady
medium loud

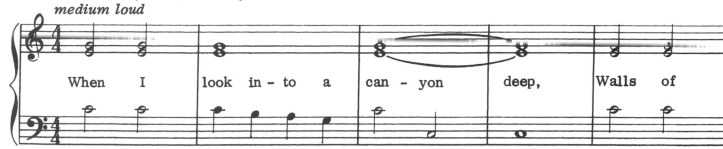

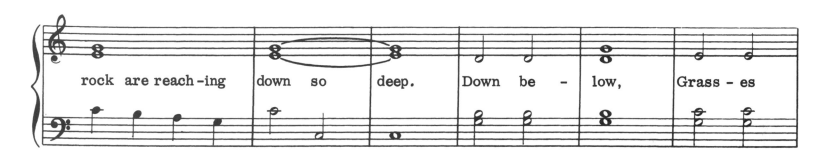

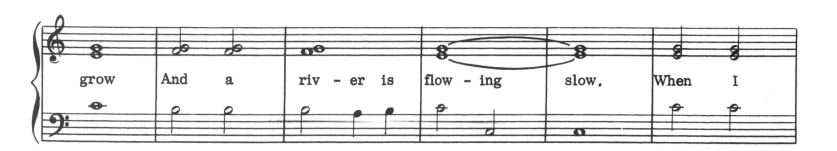

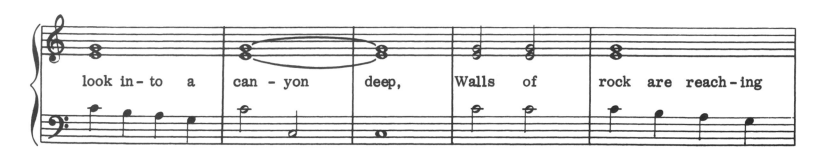

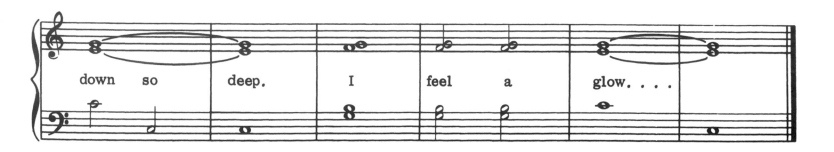

The student is ready to play this piece when he has reached page 16 of
Edna Mae Burnam's STEP BY STEP - Book Two.

STAINED GLASS WINDOW IN A CHURCH

BY EDNA MAE BURNAM

Softly and sweetly

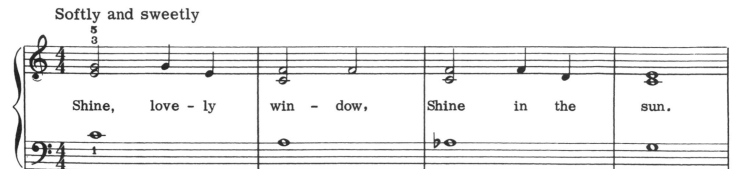

Shine, love - ly win - dow, Shine in the sun.

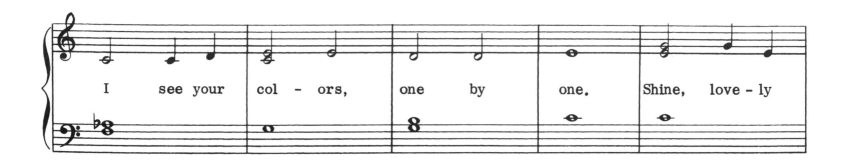

I see your col - ors, one by one. Shine, love - ly

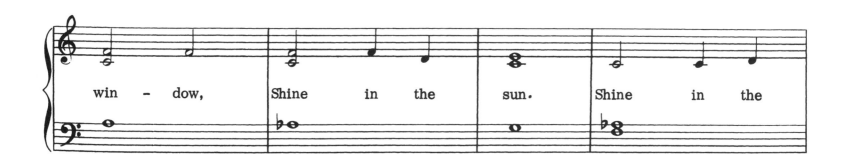

win - dow, Shine in the sun. Shine in the

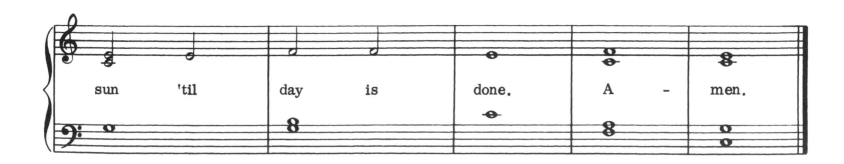

sun 'til day is done. A - men.

The student is ready to play this piece when he has reached page 19 of
Edna Mae Burnam's STEP BY STEP – Book Two.

THE SHOEMAKER

BY EDNA MAE BURNAM

5/6

Moderately fast, busy and steady
Using sewing machine

medium loud

Hammering

Hammering and shaping shoes

louder here

medium loud

The student is ready to play this piece when he has reached page 25 of
Edna Mae Burnam's STEP BY STEP – Book Two.

CANDLES

BY EDNA MAE BURNAM

Moderately fast
medium loud

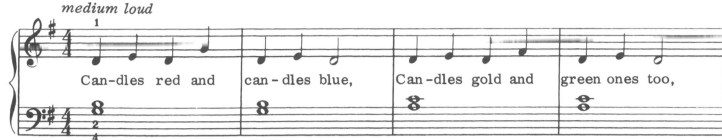

Can-dles red and   can-dles blue,   Can-dles gold and   green ones too,

Some are high, and   some are low,   But the best I   know - Are the

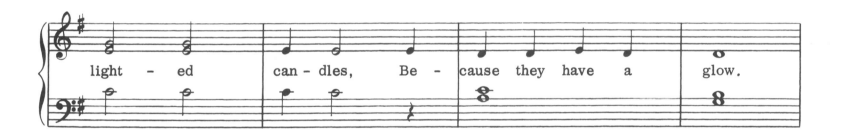

light - ed   can - dles,   Be - cause they have a   glow.

Candle flame flickers as the candle is burning -

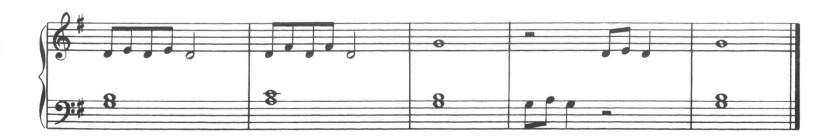

*The student is ready to play this piece when he has reached page 30 of
Edna Mae Burnam's STEP BY STEP – Book Two.*

WATCHING AN ICE SKATER

BY EDNA MAE BURNAM

Moderately fast, like a waltz
light and free

The student is ready to play this piece when he has reached page 33 of
Edna Mae Burnam's STEP BY STEP - Book Two.

SUNSET

BY EDNA MAE BURNAM

Languid, with a rocking motion in the left hand

The student is ready to play this piece when he has reached page 35 of
Edna Mae Burnam's STEP BY STEP - Book Two.

A GARDEN

BY EDNA MAE BURNAM

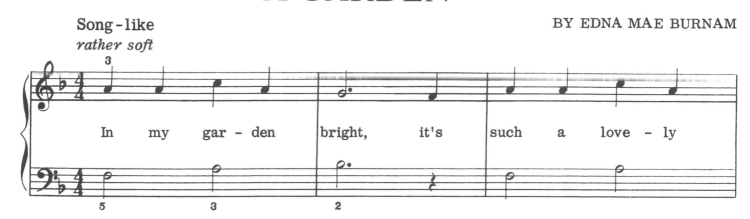

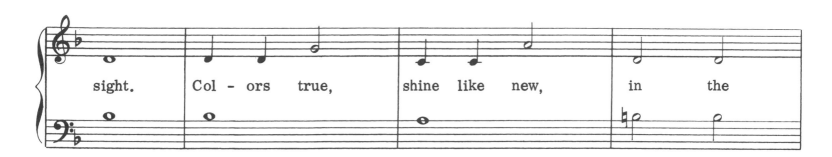

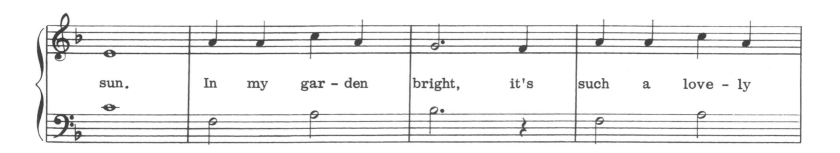

The student is ready to play this piece when he has reached page 41 of
Edna Mae Burnam's STEP BY STEP – Book Two.

HOLIDAY TIME

BY EDNA MAE BURNAM

Happy and lively

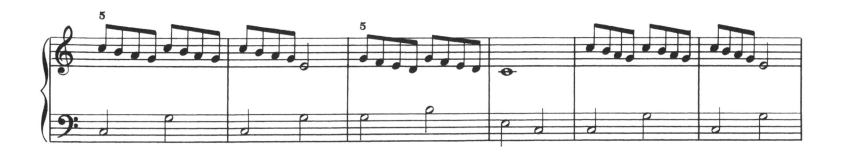

Certificate of Merit

This is to certify that

_____

has successfully completed

PIECES TO PLAY

BOOK TWO

BY

EDNA MAE BURNAM

and is now eligible for promotion to

PIECES TO PLAY

BOOK THREE

_____Teacher

Date _____

Edna Mae Burnam

Edna Mae Burnam (1907–2007) is one of the most respected names in piano pedagogy. She began her study of the instrument at age seven with lessons from her mother, and went on to major in piano at the University of Washington and Chico State Teacher's College in Los Angeles. In 1935, she sold "The Clock That Stopped"—one of her original compositions still in print today—to a publisher for $20. In 1937, Burnam began her long and productive association with Florence, Kentucky-based Willis Music, who signed her to her first royalty contract. In 1950, she sent manuscripts to Willis for an innovative piano series comprised of short and concise warm-up exercises—she drew stick figures indicating where the "real" illustrations should be dropped in. That manuscript, along with the original stick figures, became the best-selling *A Dozen a Day* series, which has sold more than 25 million copies worldwide; the stick-figure drawings are now icons.

Burnam followed up on the success of *A Dozen a Day* with her *Step by Step Piano Course*. This method teaches students the rudiments of music in a logical order and manageable pace, for gradual and steady progress. She also composed hundreds of individual songs and pieces, many based on whimsical subjects or her international travels. These simple, yet effective learning tools for children studying piano have retained all their charm and unique qualities, and remain in print today in the Willis catalog. Visit **www.halleonard.com** to browse all available piano music by Edna Mae Burnam.

A DOZEN A DAY
by
Edna Mae Burnam

The **Dozen a Day** books are universally recognized as one of the most remarkable technique series on the market for all ages! Each book in this series contains short warm-up exercises to be played at the beginning of each practice session, providing excellent day-to-day training for the student. The audio CD is playable on any CD player and features fabulous backing tracks by Ric Iannone. For Windows® and Mac computer users, the CD is enhanced so you can access MIDI files for each exercise and adjust the tempo.

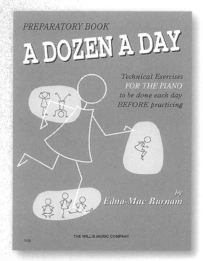

PREPARATORY BOOK
00414222 Book Only $3.95
00406476 Book/CD Pack $8.95
00406479 CD Only $9.95
00406477 Book/GM Disk Pack .. $13.95
00406480 GM Disk Only................$9.95

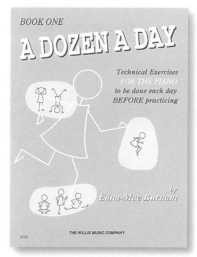

BOOK 1
00413366 Book Only $3.95
00406481 Book/CD Pack $8.95
00406483 CD Only $9.95
00406482 Book/GM Disk Pack .. $13.90
00406484 GM Disk Only................$9.95

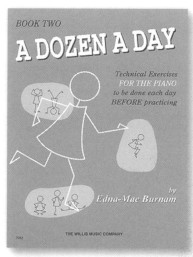

BOOK 2
00413826 Book Only $3.95
00406485 Book/CD Pack $8.95
00406487 CD Only $9.95
00406486 Book/GM Disk Pack .. $13.90
00406488 GM Disk Only................$9.95

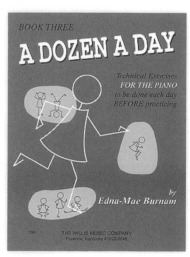

BOOK 3
00414136 Book Only $4.95
00416760 Book/CD Pack $9.95

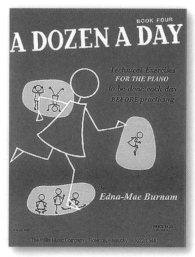

BOOK 4
00415686 Book Only $5.95
00416761 Book/CD Pack $10.95

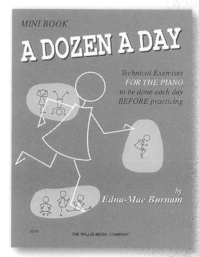

MINI BOOK
00404073 Mini Book $3.95
00406472 Book/CD Pack $8.95
00406474 CD Only $9.95
00406473 Book/GM Disk Pack .. $13.90
00406475 GM Disk Only................$9.95

WILLIS MUSIC

EXCLUSIVELY DISTRIBUTED BY
HAL•LEONARD®

Prices, contents, and availability subject to change without notice. Prices listed in U.S. funds.